<u>Frugal Cook</u>
<u>Beans</u>

50 Easy Frugal Cooking With Beans Recipes For Breakfast, Lunches, Dinners, And Snacks, Using Dry & Canned Beans That Are Simple And Incredibly Mouthwatering!

Sarah Brooks

Copyright © 2015 Sarah Brooks

STOP!!! Before you read any further....Would you like to know the secrets of Anti-Aging?

If your answer is yes, then you are not alone. Thousands of people are looking for the secret to reducing wrinkles, looking younger, and maintaining a youthful appearance.

If you have been searching for these answers without much luck, you are in the right place!

Not only will you gain incredible insight in this book, but because I want to make sure to give you as much value as possible, right now for a limited time you can get full **100% FREE access to a VIP bonus EBook** entitled **Anti-Aging Made Easy!**

Just Go Here For Free Instant Access:

www.LuxyLifeNaturals.com

Legal Notice

Disclaimer Notice

Table Of Contents

Introduction

I want to thank you and congratulate you for purchasing the book, ***Frugal Cooking With Beans.***

This "Frugal Cooking with Beans" book contains helpful hints on how to make healthy filling bean meals that won't cost you a fortune. It's packed with helpful information that will turn you into a bean convert in no time. From the different kinds of beans, to tips on how to freeze make ahead meals, this book has you covered.

There's also 50 easy bean recipes that you can easily make in your own home. Whether you're preparing for breakfast, lunch, dinner, or even snacks, you can make sumptuous bean meals in a flash.

Thanks again for purchasing this book, I hope you enjoy it!

Chapter 1: Benefits Of Frugal Cooking With Beans

Beans make a great addition to your everyday meal planning. Aside from the health benefits they provide, beans can also be made into a wide array of dishes for only a few dollars.

Beans are easy to cook if you will be using the canned variety. Just heat through for a couple of minutes, add a few more ingredients and you're ready to serve a flavorful meal.

You can also use the beans to substitute meat in your meals. Therefore, instead of buying 1 pound of beef to use for your chili recipe for example, you can just buy half a pound and add beans instead. This way, you cut down on your food cost and it is probably a lot healthier too.

And the best thing about beans? Well, they are very affordable. Just cook a large batch of dried beans, freeze and take it out whenever you need it in your dish.

Whether you choose canned or dried beans, you are sure to save a lot of money on your food budget when you cook with beans.

Chapter 2: What Type Of Beans To Use?

Thinking of adding more beans and other legumes to your diet, but don't know where to start? Then let this list be your guide.

Black beans (aka turtle beans)

Soups, stews, rice dishes and Latin American cuisines

Chickpeas (aka garbanzos)

Casseroles, hummus, minestrone soup, and Spanish and Indian dishes

Fava beans (aka broad beans)

Side dishes and stews

Red kidney beans

Chili, stews, salads, and rice dishes

Pinto beans

Soups and Southwestern dishes

Black-eyed peas (aka cowpeas)

Casseroles, salads and Southwestern dishes

Lentils

Stews, soups, salads, side dishes and Middle Eastern dishes

Adzuki beans (aka field peas)

Soups, Japanese and Chinese dishes

Lima beans (aka butter beans)

Casseroles, soups, and salads

White beans (aka cannellini beans)

Soups, stews, salads, and pasta dishes

Chapter 3: Health Benefits Of Beans

Beans and lentils are believed to be the best sources of vegetarian protein. They also contain high quality carbohydrates and are rich in different vitamins and minerals. It is no wonder that they are called the ultimate superfood.

By incorporating beans into your diet, you will be able to enjoy numerous health benefits. Here are just some of them.

Do you have problems with your heart? Beans are packed with iron, magnesium, and folate that will ensure your ticker is in tiptop shape.

Beans can also help you lose weight since these are packed with fiber that will keep you feeling fuller longer. Say goodbye to all those extra pounds, and say hello to a slimmer you.

Legumes are packed with additional vitamins and minerals like vitamin B6 and Zinc. These nutrients can help fight off muscle and memory degeneration. They also contribute to healthy tissue repair.

Chapter 4: Cheap And Delicious Bean Breakfast Recipes

Breakfast Bean Burrito

Ingredients:

- 1 can black beans, drained
- 6 eggs, whisked
- 1 small red pepper, chopped
- 1 small green pepper, chopped
- 1 onion, chopped
- 2 cups shredded cheddar cheese
- Large flour tortillas
- Tomato salsa

Preparation:

In a heated pan, cook onion, red pepper, and green pepper until soft. Add black beans.

Add eggs in vegetables. If you want your eggs soft and creamy, then feel free to add a bit of butter into the filling.

Toast the tortilla and sprinkle shredded cheese on top.

When the cheese melts, spread egg in the center of the tortilla.

Fold the burrito and serve with tomato salsa.

Baked Beans on Toast

Ingredients:

- 1 can baked beans, brand of your choice
- 4 slices toast, buttered
- Salt and pepper
- Malt vinegar

Preparation:

Open a can of baked beans and heat in a pan.

Spread beans on buttered toast.

Season with salt and pepper to taste.

Drizzle a bit of malt vinegar on the beans before serving.

Ful Medammes

Ingredients:

- 2 cups fava beans, soaked overnight
- 4 cloves garlic, crushed
- 1/3 cup parsley, chopped
- 3 lemons, quartered
- Extra virgin olive oil
- Chilli flakes
- Cumin
- Any flat bread of your choice
- Salt and pepper

Preparation:

Cook beans in unsalted water until tender.

Mash beans and add garlic, cumin, and chili flakes into the mix.

Season with salt and pepper to taste.

Drizzle extra virgin olive oil before serving with flat bread.

Garnish with quartered lemon and chopped parsley.

Moroccan Broad Bean Breakfast Soup

Ingredients:

- 2 cups fava beans, soaked overnight
- 2 cloves garlic, crushed
- 4 cups water
- Extra virgin olive oil
- Cumin

- Paprika
- Sea salt

Preparation:

Cook soaked beans with crushed garlic in water until tender. Set aside the cooking water.

Transfer the beans in a food processor and add extra virgin olive oil, cumin, and salt. Puree until you get a smooth creamy texture.

In a cooking pot, cook bean puree with cooking water that was set aside earlier. Add more water if you want to have a thinner soup.

Garnish with paprika and sea salt before serving. \

Scrambled Eggs with Pinto Beans and Salsa

Ingredients:

- 2 cups pinto beans, drained
- 4 large eggs, whisked
- 1 small green bell pepper, chopped
- 4 tablespoons sour cream
- Tomato salsa

Preparation:

Sauté green bell pepper and pinto beans in pan.

Add sour cream to whisked eggs and mix.

Cook the egg mixture with the vegetables.

Serve scrambled eggs hot with tomato salsa.

Breakfast Beans and Chorizo

Ingredients:

- 1 can red kidney beans, drained
- 1 can cannellini beans, drained
- 1 jar tomato pasta sauce, brand of your choice

- 250 grams, chorizo sausage, sliced thinly
- 4 large eggs
- 2 garlic cloves, crushed
- 1 red onion, chopped
- Ground cumin
- Lime juice
- Brown sugar

Preparation:

Cook beans, garlic, onion and chorizo in pasta sauce.

Season with cumin, lime juice, and sugar once sauce has simmered.

Break eggs on top of the sauce and allow the eggs to cook sunny side up.

Black Bean Rice Bowl

Ingredients:

- 1 can black beans, drained
- 3 cups brown rice, cooked
- 1 small green onion, chopped
- 1 cup romaine lettuce, chopped
- 1 small jalapeno pepper, seeded and sliced
- Handful of fresh cilantro, chopped
- Juice of 1 small lime
- Sea salt

Preparation:

Mix beans, green onion, romaine lettuce, jalapeno pepper, fresh cilantro and lime juice in a bowl.

Top brown rice with vegetable mixture.

Season with salt to taste before serving.

Crispy Grean Beans Fry with Eggs

Ingredients:

- 1 can green beans, drained
- 3 medium sized potatoes, diced
- 4 large eggs
- 2 tablespoons extra virgin olive oil
- 2 cloves garlic, crushed
- Chili flakes
- Salt and pepper
- Paprika

Preparation:

Heat oil and fry diced potatoes in garlic until it gets crispy.

Add green beans and chili flakes.

Crack eggs into the vegetables and cover the pan.

Wait until whites are set and season with salt, pepper, and paprika to taste before serving.

Baked Spicy Beans and Eggs

Ingredients:

- 1 can cannellini beans
- 1 can chopped tomatoes
- 4 large eggs
- 3 cloves garlic, chopped
- 2 tablespoons olive oil
- Salt and pepper
- paprika
- Coriander leaves and stalks, chopped
- Toasted bread, sliced into sticks

Preparation:

Sauté garlic in olive oil.

Add beans, chopped tomatoes, and paprika.

Add eggs and allow the whites to set.

Once the whites are set, mix it all together.

Garnish with chopped coriander and season with salt and pepper to taste.

Serve with toasted bread sticks.

Fasoulia

Ingredients:

- 1 can dark red kidney beans, undrained
- 1 small can tomato paste
- 1 small onion, chopped
- 1 small jalapeno pepper, chopped
- 1 teaspoon yellow curry powder
- 2 teaspoons cumin
- 2 teaspoons olive oil
- Salt and pepper

Preparation:

Sauté onions, jalapeno pepper, cumin, and curry powder in oil.

Add kidney beans with liquid and tomato paste. Allow to simmer.

Season with salt and pepper to taste before serving.

Breakfast Quesadilla

Ingredients:

- 1 cup black beans, drained
- ½ cup corn, drained
- 2 large eggs
- 2 egg whites
- 1 cup cheddar cheesed, shredded
- 1 small red onion, chopped
- ½ tablespoon taco seasoning
- Tomato salsa
- 4 pcs. Tortilla bread

Preparation:

Whisk egg and egg whites together. Cook scrambled.

Mix black beans, corn, onion, cheese, scrambled eggs and taco seasoning in a bowl.

Spoon mixture in the middle of each tortilla and fold.

Serve hot with tomato salsa on the side

Bean, Cheese and Ham Frittata

Ingredients:

- 1 can green beans, drained
- 1 white onion, chopped
- 4 slices deli ham, sliced into thin strips
- 4 large eggs
- 2 tablespoon olive oil
- 1 cup cream cheese, cubed
- Salt and pepper

Preparation:

Sauté white onion in olive oil until soft.

Add green beans and deli ham

In a bowl, whisk eggs, cheese and season with salt and pepper to taste.

Add eggs to pan. Make sure that the mixture is distributed evenly.

Allow to cook until edges set.

Transfer the pan to oven and bake the frittata for 25 minutes, or until the center sets.

Cut into 4 wedges before serving.

Chapter 5: Frugal Bean Lunch Recipes

Hearty White Bean Soup

Ingredients:

- 1 can cannellini beans, drained
- 1 can tomato chunks
- 5 cups vegetable stock
- 1 small onion, chopped
- 2 garlic cloves, minced
- 1 stalk celery, sliced
- 2 carrots, cubed
- 2 tablespoon olive oil
- 1 tablespoon sage, chopped
- 2 teaspoons dried oregano
- Salt and pepper

Preparation:

Sauté onion, celery, and garlic in olive oil. Add dried oregano, sage, tomato chunks. Cook until soup simmers.

Add cannellini beans, carrots, and vegetable stock and cook until carrots are soft. Stir occasionally.

Season with salt and pepper to taste before serving.

Bean Stew with Spinach and Peppers

Ingredients:

- 1 can kidney beans, drained
- 1 can tomatoes, chopped
- 1 bunch spinach, washed and chopped
- 1 medium sized red pepper, sliced into strips
- 1 small onion, sliced
- 2 garlic cloves, crushed
- 2 tablespoon olive oil

- ½ cup pitted olives
- 1 tablespoon fresh thyme, chopped
- Salt and pepper

Preparation:

Sauté onion and garlic in olive oil. Add thyme and cook until garlic turns to light brown

Add tomatoes, red pepper and olive oil. Cook for 20 minutes or so to allow flavors to develop.

Add spinach and beans. Cook for about 5 minutes or until beans start to soften.

Season with salt and pepper to taste.

Mushroom and Bean Cream Soup

Ingredients:

- 1 can white beans, drained
- 1 can mushrooms, drained and chopped
- 4 cups vegetable stock
- 1 small onion, chopped
- 2 cloves garlic, minced
- 1 teaspoon dried basil
- 1 tablespoon olive oil
- 1 tablespoon butter
- 1 tablespoon flour
- ½ cup cream
- Salt and pepper

Preparation·

Sauté onion and garlic in olive oil.

Add mushrooms and cook until garlic turns golden.

Add flour. Make sure that it coats the mushrooms.

Add butter, beans, dried basil, and vegetable stock. Bring to a simmer.

Turn off heat and stir in cream.

Season with salt and pepper to taste before serving.

Spinach Lentil Pasta

Ingredients:

- 1 can green lentils, drained
- 1 can tomato puree
- 4 cups spinach, finely chopped
- 1medium sized onion, minced
- 3 cloves garlic, minced
- 1/2 package jumbo pasta shells (about 20 pieces)
- 1 medium size carrot, diced
- 1 celery stalk, diced
- 3 tablespoon olive oil
- 1 sprig fresh thyme, chopped
- Cayenne
- Parmesan cheese

Preparation:

Cook pasta al dente according to packet instructions.

Sauté onion and garlic in olive oil. Add celery and thyme and cook until fragrant.

Add carrot, tomato puree and lentils and bring to a simmer. Leave heat on until the carrot is cooked.

Add cayenne to taste.

Pour sauce over pasta and garnish with parmesan cheese before serving.

Cuban Bean Stew

Ingredients:

- 2 cans black beans, drained, set aside water
- 1 medium size onion, finely chopped
- 3 cloves garlic, minced
- 1 medium size green bell pepper, finely chopped
- 1 small red pepper, finely chopped
- 1 cup smoked bacon, cooked, chopped
- 2 tablespoon olive oil
- 3 tablespoon cider vinegar
- Sour cream

Preparation:

Sauté onion and garlic in oil. Add bacon and green bell pepper.

Add beans and cider vinegar. Add bean water that you set aside earlier. Bring to a boil.

Garnish with red pepper bits and a dollop of sour cream before serving.

Vegetarian Express Chili

Ingredients:

- 1 can black beans, drained
- 1 can red kidney beans, drained
- 1 can pinto beans, drained
- 1 can crushed tomatoes
- 2 medium size white onions, chopped
- 3 large garlic cloves, chopped
- 1 cup water
- 5 tablespoon olive oil
- 1 tablespoon chilli powder
- 1 tablespoon cumin powder
- ½ teaspoon chipotle chilli powder
- Pinch of cinnamon
- Salt and pepper

Instructions:

Sauté onions and garlic in oil for around 5 minutes.

Mix chili powder, cumin powder and cook for 1 minute

Add crushed tomatoes and bring to a simmer.

Add beans, water, chipotle chili powder, and pinch of cinnamon. Bring to a boil and simmer uncovered. Stir occasionally.

When the sauce thickens, season with salt and pepper before serving.

Italian Bean Salad

Ingredients:

- 1 can borlotti beans, drained
- 1 can cannellini beans, drained
- 2 large tomatoes, finely chopped
- 1 small red onion, diced
- 2 garlic cloves, crushed
- 1 red chilli, deseeded and finely chopped
- 1 celery stalk, finely chopped
- 5 tablespoons olive oil
- 1 tablespoon red wine vinegar
- ¼ cup parsley, chopped

Preparation:

Sauté onions, garlic, chili, and celery in oil. Cook until onions and celery are soft.

Stir in beans and cook until heated through. Set aside to cool.

Stir in chopped tomatoes, vinegar and parsley. Serve warm.

Chickpea and Black Bean Salad

Ingredients:

- 1 can chickpeas, drained
- 1 can black beans, drained
- 1 can corn kernels, drained

- 1 bell pepper, diced
- 2 small red onions, sliced
- 5 tablespoons vegetable oil
- 3 tablespoons lime juice
- 1 teaspoon grated lime rind
- 1 teaspoon chilli powder
- 1 teaspoon granulated sugar
- 2 sprigs fresh coriander, chopped

Preparation:

In a large bowl, mix first 5 ingredients together.

Whisk together vegetable oil, lime juice, lime rind, chili powder, and sugar in a separate bowl.

Toss salad with dressing.

Garnish with coriander before serving.

Black Bean Party Salad

- 1 can black beans, drained
- 1 can corn, drained
- 1 medium onion, minced
- 2 cloves garlic, minced
- 2 red bell peppers, diced
- 1 avocado, diced
- 4 tablespoons extra virgin olive oil
- 3 tablespoons lime juie
- 1 tablespoon sugar
- 2 teaspoons salt
- Pinch of cayenne
- 1 sprig fresh cilantro, chopped

Instructions:

Combine all ingredients in a large bowl and mix well.

Chill for an hour before serving.

Bean Confetti Salad

Ingredients:

- 1 can kidney beans, drained
- 1 can garbanzo beans, drained
- 1 can black beans, drained
- 1 can corn, drained
- 2 garlic cloves, minced
- 1/2 cup balsamic vinegar
- 1/4 cup olive oil
- 1 teaspoon chili powder
- 1/2 teaspoon sugar
- 1/2 cup minced fresh cilantro
- 1/2 cup chopped sweet red pepper
- 1/2 cup chopped green pepper
- 1/4 cup chopped onion
- 1 small jalapeno pepper, seeded and finely chopped

Preparation:

In a large bowl, mix beans, corn, peppers, onion, cilantro and jalapeño.

In a smaller bowl, whisk the oil, vinegar, chili powder and sugar.

Toss vegetables in dressing to coat.

Chill before serving.

Simple Bean Salad with Pita

Ingredients:

- 1 can pinto beans, drained
- 1 cup cherry tomatoes, quartered
- 1 cucumber, peeled and diced
- 1 cup romaine lettuce, sliced
- 2 sprigs fresh parsley, chopped
- 2 tablespoons fresh mint, chopped
- 2 cloves garlic, chopped
- 2 tablespoons lemon juice

- 1 tablespoon cumin
- 3 tablespoons extra-virgin olive oil
- Salt and pepper
- 2 medium whole-wheat pita breads, torn into bite size pieces

Preparation:

Mix beans, tomatoes, cucumber, and lettuce in a serving bowl.

Whisk olive oil, lemon juice, cumin, and garlic to make dressing.

Heat pita bread until crisp.

Pour dressing over vegetables and add pita pieces

Garnish with parsley and mint before serving. Season with salt and pepper to taste.

Pasta e Fagioli

- Ingredients:
- 2 cans cannelloni beans, drained
- 1 can peeled plum tomatoes, crushed
- 1 pound cooked ditalini pasta, cooking water reserved
- 5 tablespoons cup olive oil
- 2 cloves garlic, minced
- 1/8 teaspoon chili flakes
- Salt and pepper

Preparation:

Sauté garlic and chili flakes in oil until garlic gets color.

Add crushed tomatoes and simmer for 5 minutes.

Stir in beans and pasta cooking water and bring to a boil

Add cooked pasta.

Season with salt and pepper before serving.

Greek Pasta with White Beans

Ingredients:

- 1 can cannellini beans, drained
- 2 cans diced tomatoes
- 1 pound penne pasta, cooked
- 1 cup fresh spinach, chopped
- ½ cup feta cheese, crumbled

Preparation:

Cook tomatoes and beans in a large skillet and bring to a boil. Let the sauce simmer for 10 minutes.

Add spinach and stir constantly until spinach wilts.

Pour sauce over cooked pasta and garnish with feta cheese.

Chapter 6: Bean Dinners Recipes On A Budget

Baked Beans with Sausage

Ingredients:

- 2 cans navy beans, drained
- 3 sausage links of your choice, cooked, halved lengthwise
- 2 tablespoons tomato paste
- 1 tablespoon molasses
- 1/2 cup water
- 1 medium onion, chopped
- 1 tablespoon canola oil
- 4 cups chopped collard greens, tough stems removed
- 1/2 cup barbecue sauce
- salt and pepper

Preparation:

Cook onion and collard greens in oil until wilted.

Add sausage and cook for about 3 minutes

Whisk barbecue sauce, tomato paste, water, molasses in a bowl.

Add beans and sauce into the pan. Cook for another 3 minutes, or until heated through.

Season with salt and pepper before serving.

Mexican Pinto Bean Fry

Ingredients:

- 1 can pinto beans, drained
- 8 medium size corn tortillas
- 4 large eggs
- 1 small red onion, chopped
- 3 cloves garlic, minced

- 3 tablespoons chilli powder
- 3 tablespoons canola oil
- 1 teaspoon sugar
- 1 ½ cup water
- ½ cup cheddar cheese, grated

Preparation:

Sauté garlic and chili powder in oil until garlic is cooked.

Stir in sugar, beans, and water and bring to a simmer.

While cooking the sauce, toast tortilla until crisp.

Crack eggs into sauce. Cover the sauce to allow the whites to set and cook.

Serve with crispy tortilla and cheddar cheese.

Summer Vegetable Stew

Ingredients:

- 1 can chickpeas, drained
- 1 can red lentils, drained
- 1 medium sized butternut squash, peeled and seeded, diced
- 1 large onion, chopped
- 2 large carrots, peeled, diced
- 4 cups vegetable broth
- 2 tablespoons tomato paste
- 1 small ginger, peeled, minced
- Salt and pepper

Preparation:

Combine all ingredients (except salt and pepper) in a large pot.

Cook on low with lid on until the beans are tender and start to break down.

Season with salt and pepper before serving.

White Beans and Olives Pasta

Ingredients:

- 1 can cannellini beans, drained
- 250 grams ziti pasta, cooked
- 2 ripe medium tomatoes, diced
- 1 large clove garlic, minced
- 2 tablespoons black olives, chopped
- 1 tablespoon olive oil
- ¼ cup fresh basil, chopped
- 2 tablespoons parmesan cheese

Preparation:

Sauté garlic and beans in oil. Add tomatoes, olives and basil.

Mix in cooked pasta. Make sure that oil coats the pasta.

Sprinkle parmesan cheese on top before serving.

Chicken Bean Soup

Ingredients:

- 1 can great northern beans, drained
- 1 boneless skinless chicken breast, cooked, diced
- 1 medium size carrot, diced
- 1 large clove garlic, minced
- 5 cups chicken broth
- 1 teaspoon dried rosemary
- 1 cup baby spinach, chopped
- 1/3 cup fresh basil leaves, chopped
- Croutons
- Salt and pepper

Preparation:

Sauté garlic and rosemary with the chicken and carrot.

Add beans, dried rosemary and broth and bring to a boil.

Add spinach and basil leaves and cook on low heat for 5 minutes.

Season with salt and pepper to taste.

Serve with croutons.

Rice and Lentil Dinner

Ingredients:

- 1 can red lentils, drained
- 2 cups brown rice, cooked
- 2 tablespoons extra virgin oil
- 1 tablespoon Dijon mustard
- Pinch of smoked paprika
- 1 sprig of fresh parsley, shopped
- Salt and pepper

Preparation:

Whisk oil, mustard, paprika, salt and pepper in a bowl.

Add beans and rice and stir to mix.

Garnish with parsley before serving.

Cowboy Dinner

Ingredients:

- 2 cans kidney beans, water set aside
- 1 pound lean ground beef
- 1 large onion, diced
- 3 cloves garlic, minced
- 2 cups mushrooms, diced
- 3 tablespoons canola oil
- 5 tablespoons taco seasoning

Preparation:

Sauté onions and garlic. Add beef and cook until brown.

Add beans, mushrooms and taco seasoning. Add water that you set aside from the beans and let it simmer for 10 minutes.

Bean and Barley Stew

Ingredients:

- 1 can white beans, drained
- 1 can diced tomatoes
- 6 cups vegetable broth
- ½ cup quick cooking barley
- 4 teaspoons extra virgin olive oil
- 1 medium fennel bulb, chopped
- 1 large onion, chopped
- 5 cloves garlic, crushed
- 4 cups baby spinach
- 1 teaspoon dried basil
- 2 cups parmesan cheese, grated

Preparation:

Sauté fennel, onion, garlic, and basil in oil.

Add beans, tomatoes, vegetable broth and barley and bring to a boil. Stir occasionally.

Add spinach and cook until wilted.

Top with parmesan cheese before serving.

Curried Bean and Rice

Ingredients:

- 1 can brown lentils, drained
- 3 cups basmati rice, cooked
- 4 cloves of garlic, crushed
- 2 tablespoon olive oil
- 1 teaspoon fresh ginger paste
- 2 teaspoons red curry paste

Preparation:

Sauté ginger and garlic in oil. Add curry paste and cook until fragrant.

Add brown lentils and rice, and mix well.

Bean Bolognese

Ingredients:

- 1 can fava beans, drained
- 1 can diced tomatoes
- 250 grams fettuccine, cooked
- 1 small onion, chopped
- 4 cloves garlic, crushed
- 1 celery stalk, chopped
- 2 tablespoons olive oil
- 1 bay leaf
- ½ cup white wine
- 1 cup parmesan cheese, grated

Preparation:

Sauté garlic, onion, and celery in oil. Add tomatoes and bay leaf and allow to simmer for a couple of minutes.

Add beans and white wine to the sauce. Cook until it thickens.

Pour sauce over fettuccine and top with parmesan cheese before serving.

Summer Bean Sauté

Ingredients:

- 1 can white beans, drained
- 1 medium size yellow summer squash, cubed
- 1 medium zucchini, sliced thinly
- 1 medium onion, sliced
- 2 cloves garlic, crushed
- 1 tablespoon extra-virgin olive oil
- 1 teaspoon dried oregano

- 2 medium tomatoes
- 1 tablespoon red wine vinegar
- 1 cup parmesan cheese, grated

Preparation:

Sauté garlic and onion in oil. Add zucchini and summer squash and cook until vegetables are soft.

Add beans, tomatoes, and red wine vinegar. Add dried oregano and allow to simmer.

Top with Parmesan cheese before serving.

Curry Lentils

Ingredients:

- 1 can red lentils, drained
- 8 cups chicken broth
- 1 large onion, chopped
- 3 cloves garlic, minced
- 1 small ginger, minced
- 1 tablespoon canola oil
- 2 tablespoons curry powder
- 2 bay leaves
- 2 tablespoon lemon juice
- 1/3 cup plain yogurt

Preparation:

Sauté onion, garlic, curry powder, and ginger in oil.

Add lentils, chicken broth, and bay leaves. Bring to a boil, then allow to simmer for 10 minutes.

Drizzle plain yogurt on top before serving.

Classic Bean Pasta

Ingredients:

- 1 can cannellini beans, drained
- 250 grams penne pasta, cooked
- 2 cloves garlic, minced
- 1 teaspoon chili flakes
- 1 teaspoon dried oregano
- 2 tablespoons olive oil
- 4 medium sized tomatoes
- 1 small broccoli, chopped
- ½ cup freshly grated parmesan cheese

Preparation:

Sauté garlic, chili, and oregano in oil.

Add tomatoes, beans, and broccoli. Bring to a boil and simmer for 5 minutes.

Pour over penne pasta and top with parmesan cheese before serving.

Chapter 7: Bean Snack Recipes

Crispy Chickpeas

Ingredients:

- 1 can chickpeas, drained
- 4 tablespoons olive oil
- Salt
- Seasoning of your choice

Preparation:

Dry beans completely and lay them out on a baking sheet.

Drizzle olive oil and salt on beans. Make sure all beans are covered in oil.

Bake for 30 minutes at 400F until golden brown and crunchy.

Toss in seasoning before serving.

Spicy Chickpeas

Ingredients:

- 1 can chickpeas, drained
- 4 tablespoons olive oil
- 1 teaspoon cumin
- 1 teaspoon chili powder
- 1 teaspoon cayenne pepper
- ½ teaspoon sea salt

Preparation:

Dry beans completely and lay them out on a baking sheet.

Drizzle olive oil and spices on beans. Make sure all beans are covered in oil.

Bake for 30 minutes at 400F until golden brown and crunchy.

Season with salt before serving.

White Bean Dip

Ingredients:

- 1 can cannellini beans, drained
- 5 tablespoons olive oil
- 3 cloves garlic, minced
- 2 tablespoon lime juice
- ¼ cup fresh parsley, chopped
- Pita bread
- Salt and pepper

Preparation:

Place beans, garlic, olive oil, lime juice and parsley in food processor.

Puree until smooth.

Season with salt and pepper before serving with warm pita bread.

Champion Bean Dip

Ingredients:

- 1 can pinto beans, drained
- 1 cup cheddar cheese, grated
- 1 cup sour cream
- 1 package cream cheese, softened
- ½ teaspoon cumin
- 1/2 teaspoon chili powder
- ½ teaspoon cayenne
- Tortilla chips

Preparation:

In a large bowl, mash beans.

Add all ingredients except for the tortilla chips and eat in the microwave until the beans are heated through.

Serve with tortilla chips.

Ultimate Black Bean Dip

Ingredients:

- 2 cans black beans, drained
- 1 medium red onion, chopped
- 1 garlic glove, peeled
- 1 tablespoon olive oil
- 2 tablespoons balsamic vinegar
- 1 teaspoon cumin
- Salt and pepper
- Tortilla chips
- Vegetable sticks

Preparation:

Blend first 6 ingredients in a food processor.

Transfer to serving bowl and season with salt and pepper.

Serve with tortilla chips and assorted vegetable sticks.

Butter Bean Dip

Ingredients:

- 1 can butter beans, drained
- 1 garlic clove, peeled
- 5 tablespoons extra virgin olive oil
- 1 lemon, juiced
- Handful of basil leaves, chopped
- ½ teaspoon chili flakes

Preparation:

Blend all ingredients in a food processor until smooth.

Place in a bowl and serve with chips or toast.

Bacon Bean Sandwiches

Ingredients:

- 1 can baked beans
- 5 slices bread, lightly toasted
- 10 bacon strips, cooked and drained
- 1 large white onion, sliced into rings
- 5 slices American cheese

Preparation:

Place toast on baking sheet.

Spoon beans on top of bread slices.

Top with bacon, onion rings and a cheese slice.

Bake for 15-20 minutes at 350F or until cheese melts and turns to brown.

White Bean Fritters

Ingredients:

- 1 can white beans, drained
- 2 cloves garlic, chopped
- 1 small onion, chopped
- 1 sprig parsley, chopped
- 1 tablespoon white flour
- Salt and pepper
- 5 tablespoons olive oil

Preparation:

Place beans, garlic, onions, and parsley in food processor and blend until smooth.

Season with salt and pepper to taste.

Add flour and mix.

Form into fritters and fry in hot olive oil.

Baked Bean Fritters

Ingredients:

- 1 can baked beans in tomato sauce, drained, reserve sauce
- 1 cup self-raising flour
- 3 tablespoons milk
- 2 eggs, beaten
- 1 teaspoon mild curry
- 5 tablespoons olive oil

Preparation:

Blend beans, flour, milk, eggs and curry powder in a food processor.

Fry fritters in hot oil until golden brown.

Serve with tomato sauce.

Black Bean Burger Patties

Ingredients:

- 1 can black beans, drained
- 3 cloves garlic, peeled
- ½ onion, chopped
- ½ green bell pepper, chopped
- 1 egg, beaten
- 1 tablespoon chili powder
- 1 tablespoon cumin
- ½ cup bread crumbs

Preparation:

In a food processor, mash beans, bell pepper, onion, garlic egg, chili powder, and cumin together.

Mix in breadcrumbs until you get a thick paste consistency

Fry in pan as you would a normal burger.

Simple Bean Burger

Ingredients:

- 2 cans pinto beans, drained
- ½ teaspoon garlic powder
- 2 large eggs, beaten
- 1 cup dried breadcrumbs
- Salt and pepper to taste
- 4 pieces hamburger buns

Preparation:

Mash beans and add breadcrumbs, eggs, pepper and garlic powder.

Shape into patties and fry or grill according to your preference.

Serve warm on hamburger buns.

Easy Falafels

Ingredients:

- 1 can chickpeas, drained
- 1 medium size onion, chopped
- 1 egg, beaten
- 2 tablespoons dried parsley
- 1 tablespoon garlic powder
- 1 tablespoon curry powder
- ½ teaspoon black pepper, ground
- 1 tablespoon lemon juice
- ¼ cup breadcrumbs
- 5 tablespoons olive oil

Preparation:

Blend chickpeas, onion, parsley, curry powder, garlic powder, egg, lemon juice and black pepper.

Roll into balls and fry in hot oil.

Serve with pita bread and plain yogurt.

Chapter 8: Using Dry And Canned Beans

Whether you are cooking with dry or canned beans, the following tips can help ensure that you get perfectly cooked beans every single time.

1. Always soak dried beans in cold water before cooking. This will help rehydrate the beans and reduce cooking time.

2. There are 2 soak methods you can choose from. The hot soak and the quick soak. Boil the beans on high heat for a good 3 minutes and set aside for up to 4 hours for hot soak, while quick soak only requires an hour.

3. Add salt only after the beans are cooked to your liking. Adding salt too early can stop the tenderizing process.

4. If you do not have enough time to soak beans, then you can always opt for canned beans since they are already cooked prior to canning. Choose a brand that uses high quality beans.

5. Canned beans tend to get mushy if left on heat for too long. Make sure to add beans later on in the cooking process if you want to retain a certain level of crunch.

Chapter 9: Tips For Freezing Make Ahead Meals

Making meals ahead can save you a lot of time. It can also cut your meal prep time in half during the work week. It is always great to have around, whether you are feeding your family, or some extra dinner guests. If you want to get into making make ahead meals, then here are a few tips to help you get started.

1. For your first week, double your recipe when preparing your dinners. This way, you will be able to serve half and freeze the other half. In a week's time, you will have 7 days' worth of dinner you can bring out on a lazy night.

2. Store your make ahead meals in containers built for freezing. You would not want broken containers destroying a completely good meal.

3. Make sure that your meals are also stored in appropriate sized containers for 1-2 servings. This will help you portion meals and prevent waste.

4. Secure and seal your food well with Ziploc bags to avoid freezer burns.

5. Label and date your meals in the freezer so that you will be able to keep track of the meals that need to be consumed first.

Chapter 10: Mistakes To Avoid

Cooking with beans is not just cheap; they are also relatively easy to work with. However, that does not mean that you will not commit mistakes along the way. Here are just a few that you need to avoid when cooking with beans.

1. Keeping beans in the pantry for too long - Beans tend to lose nutrients and vitamins after the first year of drying. Make sure to use dried beans within the first 6 months of buying them.

2. Not letting beans soak - Most dried bean varieties require some form of soaking. The more time you set aside for soaking, the better.

3. Cooking beans in a small pan or pot - Beans need space to move around. Make sure to cook them in quality pots for them to move around.

4. Seasoning beans too much - Beans soak flavors really well so make sure that you avoid over seasoning them. Try cooking them without the salt first, then just season before serving if you think they lack in taste.

5. Cooking beans in small portions - With the extra work of soaking and boiling beans, make sure that you cook more than what is required in the recipe. Set aside the extra portion for other meals.

Conclusion

Thank you again for purchasing the book Frugal Cooking with Beans!

I am extremely excited to pass this information along to you, and I am so happy that you now have read and can hopefully implement these strategies going forward.

I hope this book was able to help you understand beans and how to include them in your everyday diet.

The next step is to get started using this information and to hopefully live a healthy and full life!

Please don't be someone who just reads this information and doesn't apply it, the recipes in this book will only benefit you if you use them!

If you know of anyone else that could benefit from the information presented here please inform them of this book.

Finally, if you enjoyed this book and feel it has added value to your life in any way, please take the time to share your thoughts and post a review on Amazon. It'd be greatly appreciated!

Thank you and good luck!

Preview Of:

Anti-Inflammatory Diet: The #1 Anti Inflammatory Recipe Guide!

<u>Anti-Inflammatory Diet</u>

Eliminate Pain, Heal Yourself, Combat Heart Disease, And Fight Inflammation Using Food!

Introduction

I want to thank you and congratulate you for purchasing the book, *"Anti Inflammatory Diet: The #1 Anti-Inflammatory Recipe Guide! - Eliminate Pain, Heal Yourself, Combat Heart Disease and Fight Inflammation Using Food"*.

This "Anti Inflammatory Diet" book contains proven steps and strategies on how to fight inflammation through holistic approach. Inflammation is the body's natural response to infection and injuries. It is essential to start the healing process. Redness, pain, swelling and heat are symptoms which mean that the body is triggering the immune system to fight foreign bodies and start tissue repair. The problem arises when the healthy cells are damaged in the aftermath of inflammation.

Inflammation is linked to major chronic illness like heart diseases, stroke and diabetes. Fortunately, people are not powerless in preventing inflammation from going out of control. By ensuring that you have a healthy lifestyle, you are relieving your body from toxins and prevent common chronic illness.

Adopting healthy habits can dramatically improve your inflammation symptoms. This is a combination of a healthy diet and good habits. Fuel your body with natural anti-inflammatory foods to keep your joints functioning well.

Take control of your life and start living a healthy lifestyle to feel better.

Thanks again for purchasing this book, I hope you enjoy it!

Chapter 1: Anti-inflammatory Diet Guidelines

Unlike other diets, the anti-inflammatory diet is different since it is solely focused on weight loss. It is more of a dietary guideline for life than a short term diet.

There are also more than one approach to the anti-inflammatory diet with each one having its own benefit. Many doctors say that the anti-inflammatory diet can benefit everyone and is good for overall health.

What is inflammation?

Inflammation is the body's response to harmful and irritating stimuli. It is the body's way of protecting itself by removing damaged cells, pathogens and irritants to encourage a faster healing process.

Inflammation is not the same as infection although infection can cause inflammation. Infection is caused by virus, fungus and bacteria while inflammation is the body's reaction to it.

Initially, inflammation is beneficial to your immune response. For example, if you cut yourself while cooking, you might notice the area swells and reddens. This response is essential in the healing process.

Types of inflammation

- Acute inflammation

Acute inflammation starts rapidly as soon as the injury is acquired. It can last for few minutes to only few days. The most common examples of acute inflammation are cuts, bruises and sore throat.

- Chronic inflammation

Chronic inflammation is long term and can even last for years. It usually results after the body has failed to eliminate the cause of acute inflammation. It is also a response to antigens. It happens when the body attacks healthy tissue because it mistakes it for harmful pathogens. Examples include asthma, tuberculosis and chronic sinusitis.

Signs of inflammation

- Pain. The inflicted area will be painful most especially when touched. Chemicals in the body are released in the nerve ending making the area much more sensitive.
- Redness. The redness happens because the capillaries are filled with more blood than usual.
- Immobility. Since the area is painful to touch, you might also experience loss of function.
- Swelling. This is caused by the accumulation of fluid in the affected area.
- Heat. More blood accumulates in the area which makes it warmer than the rest of the body.

What happens during inflammation?

You can feel the effect of inflammation immediately after the tissue is damaged. Acute inflammation occurs in three stages. First, the arterioles or the small branches of the arteries that supply blood to the different parts of the body dilate and results to an increase in blood flow. The capillaries become permeable and fluid and blood move in-between the spaces of cells. Neutrophilis which is a type of white blood cell that contains enzyme that digest microorganisms move out of the capillaries. It then transfers to the spaces between the cells.

The Neutrophilis is the body's first line of defense since it contains enzymes that can destroy bacteria and prevent infections. However, it also contains inflammatory properties which can lead to heart ailments and autoimmune disease.

Function of the anti-inflammatory diet

Physicians and medical experts may recommend anti-inflammatory diets to lessen the effect of inflammation in the body. The diet is usually prescribed with other medicines but you can also follow it to simply reduce inflammation symptoms in your system. Adding foods that improve symptoms of chronic disease supplies the body with the needed nutrients to decrease body inflammation.

Thanks For Previewing My Exciting Book Entitled:

"Anti-Inflammatory Diet: The #1 Anti Inflammatory Recipe Guide! Eliminate Pain, Heal Yourself, Combat Heart Disease, And Fight Inflammation Using Food!"

To purchase this book, simply go to the Amazon Kindle store and simply search:

"ANTI-INFLAMMATORY DIET"

Then just scroll down until you see my book. You will know it is mine because you will see my name "Sarah Brooks" underneath the title.

Alternatively, you can visit my author page on Amazon to see this book and other work I have done. Thanks so much, and please don't forget your free bonuses

DON'T LEAVE YET! - CHECK OUT YOUR FREE BONUSES BELOW!

Free Bonus Offer: Get Free Access To The www.LuxyLifeNaturals.com VIP Newsletter!

Once you enter your email address you will immediately get free access to this awesome newsletter!

But wait, right now if you join now for free you will also get free access to the "Anti-Aging Made Easy" free EBook!

To claim both your FREE VIP NEWSLETTER MEMBERSHIP and your FREE BONUS Ebook on ANTI-AGING MADE EASY!

Just Go To:

www.LuxyLifeNaturals.com

Made in the USA
Coppell, TX
26 March 2021